heav
nature sing

DEVOTIONS FOR
ADVENT & CHRISTMAS
2021–2022

 AUGSBURG FORTRESS

Minneapolis

HEAVEN AND NATURE SING
Devotions for Advent and Christmas 2021–2022

pISBN 978-1-5064-8056-5
eISBN 978-1-5064-8058-9

Writers: Laura R. Holck (November 28–December 5), Troy M. Troftgruben (December 6–15), Stacey Nalean-Carlson (December 16–22), Meghan Johnston Aelabouni (December 23–30), Ron Valadez (December 31–January 6)

Editor: Laurie J. Hanson
Cover image: Aurora borealis on the Lofoten islands, Norway. Green northern lights above mountains. Night sky with polar lights. Night winter landscape with aurora and reflection on the water surface. Norway-image iStock/Biletskiy_Evgeniy
Cover design: Alisha Lofgren
Interior design: Eileen Engebretson
Interior photos: All images © iStock. Used by permission.

The paper used in this publication meets the minimum requirements of American National Standard for Information Sciences—Permanence of Paper for Printed Library Materials, ANSI Z329.48-1984.

Manufactured in the USA.

21   1 2 3 4 5

Welcome

The story of Jesus' birth in the Gospel of Luke is filled with song. Luke begins with the news that Elizabeth and Zechariah, despite their old age, will have a son who will prepare people for the arrival of the long-awaited Messiah. This is a prelude to the singing that follows from Elizabeth and Zechariah; Jesus' mother, Mary; the prophets Simeon and Anna; and even an angel choir!

This book continues the Christian tradition of setting aside time to prepare for the celebration of Jesus' birth and to anticipate his return. The Advent season of preparation then unfolds in the joy of the twelve days of Christmas and the day of Epiphany. You will find daily devotions here for the first Sunday of Advent (November 28, 2021) through Epiphany (January 6, 2022). Each devotion features a scripture reading from Luke, accompanied by a photo, a quote to ponder, a reflection, and a prayer. The book also offers household blessings and prayers (see pages 84–94) to enrich your preparations and celebrations.

During these days of Advent and Christmas, may the good news of Jesus' birth fill our lives and our world with joy and peace. Let heaven and nature sing!

Luke 1:1-4

Since many have undertaken to set down an orderly account of
the events that have been fulfilled among us, . . . I too decided . . .
to write an orderly account for you, excellent Theophilus, so
that you may know the truth concerning the things about which
you have been instructed.

To ponder

If it is the truth, it is true all the time and everywhere, and sincere
lovers of truth will take it from wherever it comes.—Richard
Rohr,"Truth Is One"

Truth

The gospel writer Luke sets out to record the *truth* of the events of Jesus' life for the benefit of his friend Theophilus. This statement can give us pause: How do we know what is true and what is not, especially when opposing ideas claim to be true?

One test for truth might be to consider the source. After all, Luke and Theophilus are friends of some sort and we tend to trust what our friends tell us. But we also know that we make friends with people we like and who may already share our opinions, so how do we distinguish truth from mere agreement?

Even wisdom may not be a good test for the source of truth, for our sense of what is wise can also stem from other foundations, like shared experience or inspiration.

But the root of truth might be found in another question: What is life-giving? God's truth, the real truth, is rooted in a desire for the redemption and new life of all people and all creation. This deep truth never calls for violence or oppression, never takes sides, and rebukes harm of any kind. It seeks restoration, wholeness, and unity. If the gospel writer Luke sets out to record the truth of the events of Jesus' life, then in these pages we can expect to find a story of life-giving transformation that includes all people everywhere. We can expect to find a story that springs from faith for faith in our daily lives.

Prayer

God of life, may Luke's story lead us to the truth that brings new life for all people. Amen.

Luke 1:5-7

In the days of King Herod of Judea, there was a priest named Zechariah, who belonged to the priestly order of Abijah. His wife was a descendant of Aaron, and her name was Elizabeth. Both of them were righteous before God, living blamelessly according to all the commandments and regulations of the Lord. But they had no children.

To ponder

The Bible is a sacred collection of letters and laws, poetry and proverbs, philosophy and prophecies, written and assembled over thousands of years in cultures and contexts very different from our own, that tells the complex, ever-unfolding story of God's interaction with humanity.—Rachel Held Evans, *A Year of Biblical Womanhood*

Bound by love and promise

Zechariah and Elizabeth were both descended from the priestly line of Aaron and the Levites; Zechariah himself was a priest. They were righteous before God. And yet, in a day when childlessness meant social disgrace, this couple found themselves with no children.

As the biblical story about this couple begins, we sense that something is about to happen. We are ready and waiting for God to intervene. But do we hold out this hope for ourselves? Can we look into our own future with the same kind of anticipation and assurance that we feel for Zechariah and Elizabeth? It is admittedly easier to hold out hope for them because, after all, this is an ancient story, and we might already know how it turns out.

But, friends, our lives are a continuation of the same story, crafted by the same God and unfolding on the same timeline. The way God heard Zechariah and Elizabeth is the way God hears us. The way God loved them is the way God loves us. The way God was there for them is the way God is there for us. That's the witness and power of biblical stories. They are ours and we are theirs, bound by God in love and promise.

Prayer

Give us faith, faithful God, to see that our lives too are swallowed up in the victory of your love and grace. Amen.

Luke 1:8-11

Once when [Zechariah] was serving as priest before God . . . he was chosen by lot, according to the custom of the priesthood, to enter the sanctuary of the Lord and offer incense. . . . Then there appeared to him an angel of the Lord, standing at the right side of the altar of incense.

To ponder

Coincidence is God's way of remaining anonymous.—Charlotte Clemensen Taylor, "Former Chaplain Working to Found First New Order of Monks in 700 Years"

On purpose

God spoke directly to people for thousands of years. The stories of the Old Testament tell us God regularly appeared in person, sent angels and messengers, and spoke through the prophets. Until God didn't. For some reason, God stopped speaking altogether and there were no stories recorded for more than four hundred years—until this one.

When God finally chose to send an angel after centuries of apparent absence, God sent that angel to Zechariah in the temple, in the Holy of Holies, the most sacred space in all Jerusalem. Zechariah was there by chance, but the angel was not. Zechariah was chosen by lot, one of more than twenty thousand priests qualified to enter the Holy of Holies and therefore a lucky, unlikely choice, but the angel was sent by God on purpose.

God moves in an intentional circle of grace, waiting for us, sending angels and messengers to reveal a glorious promise, answer an unwavering prayer, fulfill the deepest desire of our hearts. God is not frivolous, but pursues us intentionally with a promise of love, fulfillment, rescue, delight. God's design is life and fullness, joy and promise. There are no coincidences with God. There is no lottery, and with God life is not about luck. God moves on purpose.

Prayer

Find us, O God, in our waiting places and fill us with promise and hope. Amen.

December 1

Luke 1:12-15

When Zechariah saw [the angel], he was terrified. . . . But the angel said to him, "Do not be afraid, Zechariah, for your prayer has been heard. Your wife Elizabeth will bear you a son, and you will name him John. You will have joy and gladness, and many will rejoice at his birth, for he will be great in the sight of the Lord. He . . . will be filled with the Holy Spirit."

To ponder

The Giver of all gifts asks *me* to give! . . . As if I too could body forth . . . Heaven.—Malcolm Guite, "As If"

As if

In the Holy of Holies, just to the right of the incense stand, an angel appeared. Of course Zechariah was terrified! Who wouldn't be? It's not normal, then or now, to see an angel of God, nor to hear that our prayers are heard and answered. It's not normal to hear from an angel that we will bear children, or that any one of a hundred other things that inhabit our prayers will come to pass, and that we will then be glad and rejoice.

Mostly we are consigned to faith. We tend to keep praying, hoping to see things change over time. But what if we are called to pray and behave as if we have seen the angel in the Holy of Holies, just to the right of the incense stand? What if we are called to carry Zechariah's encounter *inside us every day* and let the evidence of this encounter leak out of our lives, our words, our actions? What if the angel's proclamation of joy, gladness, and rejoicing is also given to *us*?

Then every moment, every interaction would be flooded and filled with the light and assurance of angelic presence, and we would become messengers of divine blessing.

Prayer

In the Holy of Holies, O God, Zechariah saw your messenger. May the promises of that day live inside us now, for our sake and the sake of the world. Amen.

December 2

Luke 1:16-17

[The angel said, "Your son] will turn many of the people of Israel to the Lord their God. . . . He will go before him . . . to make ready a people prepared for the Lord."

To ponder

Every human interaction offers you the chance to make things better or to make things worse.—Barbara Brown Taylor, *An Altar in the World*

Signposts

Before the age of GPS and map apps, signposts were critical to reaching one's destination. Be it a street sign in a neighborhood or a sign at an intersection in the middle of nowhere, signposts encouraged continuing in the same direction or offered course correction.

God has provided all sorts of signposts through the ages, guiding people with a burning bush, with pillars of cloud and fire, and later with a star; but most of the time God leads through the lives of other people.

The angel told Zechariah that his son would be a signpost, pointing people to God, helping them prepare for God's coming. The life of Zechariah's son would matter. By the way he lived and the choices he made, he would prepare people and prepare the way for God.

Our lives matter too. The things we do matter. The principles by which we live matter. The words we speak matter. All the things we do and say build our lives into signposts to point this way or that, to prepare a way for God—or not. Like Zechariah's son, we are living signposts who reveal God's glory to others through our everyday lives. Through the choices we make, our lives become examples of what it looks like to follow Jesus, what life in Christ is like, and what it means to be faithful during times of challenge and of celebration.

Prayer

Build us up, Lord, into signposts that reveal your glory. Amen.

Luke 1:18-20

Zechariah said to the angel, "How will I know that this is so?" . . .
The angel replied, "I am Gabriel. I stand in the presence of God,
and I have been sent to speak to you and to bring you this good
news. But now, because you did not believe my words, . . . you will
become mute, unable to speak, until the day these things occur."

To ponder

I do not at all understand the mystery of grace; only that it meets
us where we are but does not leave us where it found us. —Anne
Lamott, *Traveling Mercies*

An angelic time-out

Zechariah couldn't see the forest for the trees. God had just sent an *angel* to deliver a wild and bold promise, and Zechariah asked for a sign! Here's how you will know, Zechariah: God sent an angel to you. The angel *is* the sign.

We often miss the work God is doing in our lives because we are expecting something different. Sometimes we are looking in another direction and miss God completely. Sometimes we are trapped in the past, accustomed to the way it has always been or to having nothing happen at all. Sometimes what God brings is not what we planned, so we get mad or discount the miraculous. Our expectations about what *should* happen prevent us from fully experiencing what *is* happening.

We are more like Zechariah than we may care to admit, and frankly, the angel's response to him seems overly harsh. But the angel striking Zechariah silent is also an act of divine intervention. Zechariah is given a sort of "angelic time-out," a chance to sit on the sidelines and watch a miracle of God unfolding in his wife's abdomen and in their very lives. His inability to speak is a mystery of grace that we cannot begin to understand, but it leaves him changed forever.

Prayer

May your grace, O God, move us closer to you. Amen.

December 4

Luke 1:21-22

Meanwhile the people were waiting for Zechariah, and wondered at his delay in the sanctuary. When he did come out, he could not speak to them, and they realized that he had seen a vision in the sanctuary. He kept motioning to them and remained unable to speak.

To ponder

If you have a sacred space and use it, eventually something will happen.—Joseph Campbell with Bill Moyers, *The Power of Myth*

Encountering God

The people were waiting for Zechariah, for it was customary that the priest who burned the incense would return from the Holy of Holies with a blessing for those who had gathered. But they waited longer than usual that day, and wondered why the priest was late.

When he did show up, he didn't speak—couldn't speak! Despite his silence, they could tell by his face that he had seen a vision. He had encountered the Holy in God's house, and it had changed him.

Encounters with the Holy can change us too. They can leave us awestruck, like Zechariah. They can change the course of our lives, as Elizabeth learned. They can renew our faith and give us hope. Despair turns into joy, the broken are made whole, a way is created in our wilderness, a new day dawns.

Sometimes (maybe more often than we would wish), we don't expect anything to happen in our sanctuaries, or we are only there out of a sense of duty or obligation. But something will happen. God can and will move in our sanctuaries. We will encounter God there. God can meet us anytime and under any circumstance, and when God meets us in God's house, both we and the space are transformed.

Prayer

Bless and hallow our sanctuaries, O God, that we might expect to meet you there. Amen.

Luke 1:24-25

After those days his wife Elizabeth conceived, and for five months she remained in seclusion. She said, "This is what the Lord has done for me when he looked favorably on me."

To ponder

I have held many things in my hands, and I have lost them all; but whatever I have placed in God's hands, that I still possess.
—Martin Luther, in a letter to Justus Jonas the Elder

The gaze of God

For most of human history, the gaze of the gods—who were often seen as mischievous or vengeful—was a curse. When the gods noticed someone, that person became their plaything or the object of their aggression. To draw their attention was to risk being the target of their frustration, boredom, or anger. To avoid their punishment required sacrifices and other acts of devotion.

In Elizabeth's story we see something entirely different, as God looks favorably upon a woman who has endured barrenness her entire life. We encounter a merciful and personal God who apparently delights in the joy of an ordinary woman. God sees Elizabeth, and rather than experiencing God's wrath, she knows God's favor.

Our God is not like the gods of the ancient world. God is not vindictive, vengeful, or just plain mean. We are neither God's playthings nor the objects of God's anger or curiosity. God looks instead upon us and the world with love and care, delighting in the things that delight us and sorrowing over things that cause us pain. God enters into the heart of our suffering and challenges, bringing the promise of life and hope. God sees us, and with that gaze come attention, care, and transformation.

Prayer

Thank you, God, for seeing us. Thank you for your loving gaze. Amen.

December 6

Luke 1:26-29

In the sixth month the angel Gabriel was sent by God to a town in Galilee called Nazareth, to a virgin engaged to a man whose name was Joseph, of the house of David. The virgin's name was Mary. And he came to her and said, "Greetings, favored one! The Lord is with you." But she was much perplexed by his words and pondered what sort of greeting this might be.

To ponder

I'll just tell you this: only if there are angels in your head will you ever, possibly, see one.—Mary Oliver, "The World I Live In"

God's messengers

Most days we would welcome a visit from an angel—to guide us, help us, or give us a message from God. We may envy Mary for so direct an encounter.

But Mary did not embrace it immediately. "Much perplexed," she wondered what in the world to make of it. Apparently, even chief members of the heavenly host cannot calm our concerns instantly.

In scripture the word *angel* simply means "messenger." That is all Gabriel is: a messenger. Though he stands before God (Luke 1:19), he could have been plain-clothed and ordinary-looking.

Who are God's messengers today? We may not often encounter heavenly beings, but that doesn't mean God isn't speaking. God speaks through circumstances, scripture, and other people—plain-clothed and ordinary as they are. Who reminds you of something about God? Who tells or shows you something about God? God's messengers may be family members, neighbors, coworkers, church people, and others. In fact, they may be the last people you think of when you hear the word *angel*. And like Mary, you may not embrace them immediately. But that changes neither their role nor God's persistence. God's messengers will still show up at your doorstep, reminding you: "Greetings! The Lord is with you."

Prayer

Gracious God, help us to listen, recognize your voice, and welcome your messengers. Amen.

Luke 1:30-31

The angel said to her, "Do not be afraid, Mary, for you have found favor with God. And now, you will conceive in your womb and bear a son, and you will name him Jesus."

To ponder

Over the years I have come to realize that the greatest trap in our life is not success, popularity, or power, but self-rejection. . . . Self-rejection is the greatest enemy of the spiritual life because it contradicts the sacred voice that calls us the "Beloved." Being the Beloved expresses the core truth of our existence.—Henri J. M. Nouwen, *Life of the Beloved*

You—yes, you—are highly favored

We often think of Mary as a spiritual rock star. After all, she gave birth to the Son of God, and so is revered to this day by Christians around the world as the "Mother of God" (*Theotokos*).

But let's not forget: at this point in her story, Mary had done *nothing* significant. She had no credentials. She had no connections. She was no pillar of faith. Mary would have been seen as a young, poor, insignificant nobody.

But God saw her very differently. Not only is the Lord with her; Gabriel also tells Mary, not once but twice, that she's favored by God (Luke 1:28, 30). Though a nobody to society, Mary is "highly favored" by the Creator of all.

God sees you similarly: favored, special, cherished, beloved. Whoever you are to others, you are profoundly dear to God. It doesn't matter whether you believe it. (Mary probably didn't.) It doesn't matter whether you've done anything great. (Mary hadn't.) God is deeply fond of you. To God, you are one of a kind, highly favored, and especially loved. And there is nothing you can do to change it—to make God love you any less or any more.

In worship, the sacraments, and the scriptures, God in Christ says: "You—yes, you—are highly favored."

Prayer

O Creator, Redeemer, and Lover of our souls, remind and convince us that you cherish us. Embrace us and let us rest perfectly in your love. Amen.

December 8

Luke 1:32-33

[The angel said,] "He will be great, and will be called the Son of the Most High, and the Lord God will give to him the throne of his ancestor David. He will reign over the house of Jacob forever, and of his kingdom there will be no end."

To ponder

I have a dream that my four little children will one day live in a nation where they will not be judged by the color of their skin but by the content of their character. I have a dream today.—Martin Luther King Jr., "Speech at Bishop Charles Mason Temple"

Jesus shall reign

Many of us have deep political convictions. They are shaped by our age, upbringing, experiences, education, finances, demographics, race, friendship circles, and religious faith. And even though our long-term goals are shared by other political parties (at least in theory), it's often a stretch for us to appreciate their worldviews as faithful.

Political convictions were no less entrenched in Jesus' day. Under Roman rule, Jewish people responded in passionate ways—from acceptance to resistance, and from religious cooperation to militant extremism. In this atmosphere, Gabriel's promise of an everlasting kingdom under "the Son of the Most High" was loaded language. He spoke of a Messiah greater than any ruler the world has known.

This season of Advent, in a world divided by race, partisanship, convictions, and creeds, we pray for the reign of Jesus to be made known among us today.

Prayer

O come, O King of nations, come, O Cornerstone that binds in one: / refresh the hearts that long for you; restore the broken, make us new. / Rejoice! Rejoice! Emmanuel shall come to you, O Israel. ("O come, O come, Emmanuel," ELW 257)

December 9

Luke 1:34-37

Mary said to the angel, "How can this be, since I am a virgin?" The angel said to her, "The Holy Spirit will come upon you, and the power of the Most High will overshadow you; therefore the child to be born will be holy; he will be called Son of God. And now, your relative Elizabeth in her old age has also conceived a son. . . . For nothing will be impossible with God."

To ponder

Keep some room in your heart for the unimaginable.—Mary Oliver, "Evidence (1)"

The God who makes the impossible possible

Mary is right to ask questions. Her questions, unlike Zechariah's, are more practical than skeptical. In response, Gabriel promises a miracle by the Holy Spirit—like the miracle already at work in Elizabeth. Only God can create life out of nothing. Clearly these changes for Elizabeth and Mary are God's handiwork. As Gabriel points out, "nothing will be impossible with God."

Even as a young girl, a friend of mine felt called to ministry. At the Lutheran church she attended, she often stood in the pulpit with the strange sense that she was supposed to be there. But at that time no Lutheran church ordained women. Her call was impossible. She felt ashamed for feeling it.

But in unforeseeable ways, doors opened. My friend became a deaconess, then, when the church allowed it, a pastor. Then she earned a PhD and became one of the first female professors at a Lutheran seminary. At one time obstacles made her path impossible. But then nothing is impossible with God.

Obstacles abound to our God-given hopes and dreams. But no obstacle is too hard or too great for the God who makes the impossible possible.

Prayer

All-powerful God, in Christ you create life and make all things new. Continue to make known your life-giving work among us. Amen.

Luke 1:38

Then Mary said, "Here am I, the servant of the Lord; let it be with me according to your word." Then the angel departed from her.

To ponder

The world says, "When you were young you were dependent and could not go where you wanted, but when you grow old you will be able to make your own decisions, go your own way, and control your own destiny." But Jesus has a different vision of maturity: It is the ability and willingness to be led where you would rather not go.—Henri J. M. Nouwen, *In the Name of Jesus*

Surrender

Mary is a model of faith for one simple reason: she said "yes" to God.

Mary's response is short and sweet. It's even more to the point in Greek—just thirty-nine letters (ten words). She says: "I'm the Lord's servant—your word be done" (my paraphrase).

We often associate great faith with doing great things. But the greatest acts of faith are ones of surrender, openness, and simply opening our hands to receive. Mary embodies this faith beautifully. With her, we pray: "I'm your servant, God; your word be done."

Prayer

My Lord God, I have no idea where I am going. I do not see the road ahead of me. I cannot know for certain where it will end. Nor do I really know myself, and the fact that I think that I am following your will does not mean that I am actually doing so. But I believe that the desire to please you does in fact please you. And I hope I have that desire in all that I am doing. I hope that I will never do anything apart from that desire. And I know that if I do this you will lead me by the right road, though I may know nothing about it. Therefore will I trust you always, though I may seem to be lost and in the shadow of death. I will not fear, for you are ever with me, and you will never leave me to face my perils alone. (Thomas Merton, *Thoughts in Solitude*)

Luke 1:39-41

In those days Mary set out and went with haste to a Judean town in the hill country, where she entered the house of Zechariah and greeted Elizabeth. When Elizabeth heard Mary's greeting, the child leaped in her womb.

To ponder

Joy is the serious business of heaven.—C. S. Lewis, *Letters to Malcolm*

Responses of joy

Responses of joy are an underappreciated spiritual practice. They are also contagious.

A friend of mine entered graduate school in hopes of a career. His newlywed wife supported him in school. At the end of his program, he was offered his dream job. Hearing that, his wife leaped for joy into his arms. To this day, he cherishes the moment as one of the best in his life.

At Mary's arrival, Elizabeth's child leaped for joy. No biological reason adequately explains this. Somehow, mysteriously, the future herald of Jesus (John the baptizer) recognized the presence of greatness—even in the womb. And the response? An act of unbridled joy.

Kids are better at joy than adults. Burdened by social norms and responsibilities, adults often find it hard to cut loose with joy. And they miss out. In this, we adults have a lot to learn from children. Kids experience and express joy in ways that reflect the joyfulness of God.

Joy is incomplete until it is expressed. Joy is related to gratitude, which runs deeper than passing circumstances or feelings of happiness. Joy is finally grounded in celebrating God's goodness to us. What brings you joy these days? How do you express it? What would it take for you to dance or shout—or leap—for joy?

Prayer

Gracious God, grant us a joy that is rooted in your goodness, reflective of your love, and enriching to our lives. Let your Holy Spirit nurture in us a joy in Christ that endures and outshines the obstacles and misfortunes of life. Amen.

Luke 1:41-45

And Elizabeth was filled with the Holy Spirit and exclaimed with a loud cry, "Blessed are you among women, and blessed is the fruit of your womb. And why has this happened to me, that the mother of my Lord comes to me? For as soon as I heard the sound of your greeting, the child in my womb leaped for joy. And blessed is she who believed that there would be a fulfillment of what was spoken to her by the Lord."

To ponder

Faith is to believe what you do not see; the reward of this faith is to see what you believe.—Augustine, *Sermons* 4.1.1

Faith in the unseen

Elizabeth speaks three blessings: one on Mary, one on her child, and one on Mary *for believing* the Lord's word. These blessings are not random outbursts: they come from a woman "filled with the Holy Spirit."

People have written thick books on faith, but Elizabeth tells us all we need to know: Faith is simply believing that God's word is true. Further, it's believing that God's word is true *for you*. Faith is not understanding; it's receiving. Faith is not doing; it's acceptance. Faith is about letting go and trusting someone else to be true to their word.

One summer in Europe, I contacted a friend in the Netherlands for a visit. He gave me his address, inviting me to find him. When I arrived in town, I realized the act of faith this was. I didn't speak Dutch. I had never visited the country. What if I got lost? What if he wasn't home? What if I couldn't find him? . . . In the end, I found him: waiting, happy to see me, and ready to search for me if I was lost.

Faith is trusting that God will not fail you. God says, "I forgive you," "I will guide you," "I have plans for you," "I love you." Faith is trusting that God's word is true *for you*.

Prayer

Lord, I believe; help my unbelief. Amen. (Mark 9:24)

December 13

Luke 1:46-49

"My soul magnifies the Lord,
and my spirit rejoices in God my Savior, for he has looked with
favor on the lowliness of his servant.
Surely, from now on all generations will call me blessed;
for the Mighty One has done great things for me,
and holy is his name."

To ponder

Those who sing praise do not just praise, but also praise joyfully.
Those who sing praise do not just sing, but also love the One
to whom they are singing. In the praise of those who confess is
public proclamation, and in the song of those who love is loving
affection.—Augustine, *Exposition of the Psalms 72:1*

The one who sings prays twice

The Roman Catholic Church's catechism includes the saying "The one who sings prays twice" (*bis orat qui cantat*). Sometimes credited to Augustine, it is at best loosely based on the longer quote above ("To ponder"). But the saying still rings true: sung prayer is somehow richer, deeper, more profound.

In today's text, Mary begins a song called the *Magnificat* (Latin for "magnifies"). She enters a long legacy of biblical women who praise God's victories in song (Miriam, Deborah, Hannah). These women don't just sing songs—they are active agents in God's victories. And their songs focus not on themselves, but on God.

Do you sing praise to God? When? What songs? You don't need great talent to hum along, to join in somehow, or to find beauty in music.

My father rarely attended church. But a memory I cherish is how he sang at Christmas Eve worship. His voice wasn't terribly refined, but to my ears, it was beautiful. To God's ears, your voice is the same. Along with Mary, try singing some praise to God.

Prayer

My soul proclaims your greatness, Lord; I sing my Savior's praise! / You looked upon my lowliness, and I am full of grace. / Now ev'ry land and ev'ry age this blessing shall proclaim— / great wonders you have done for me, and holy is your name. ("My soul proclaims your greatness," ELW 251)

Luke 1:50-53

"His mercy is for those who fear him
from generation to generation.
He has shown strength with his arm;
he has scattered the proud in the thoughts of their hearts.
He has brought down the powerful from their thrones,
and lifted up the lowly;
he has filled the hungry with good things,
and sent the rich away empty."

To ponder

True peace is not merely the absence of tension; it is the presence of justice.—Martin Luther King Jr., "When Peace Becomes Obnoxious"

A Jesus for justice

At Christmastime, we imagine Jesus as a gentle baby. But Mary's song shows us a different vision. This Jesus will carry out God's purposes of scattering the proud, dethroning the powerful, exalting the humiliated, and bankrupting the rich. Imagine these claims as a political platform today. They are hardly "gentle" to the status quo!

Mary's song resonates with that of Hannah (1 Samuel 2:1-10), who prayed for a son and then dedicated him to God. Mary's song also reflects a rich tradition of prophetic calls for justice in scripture. Prophetic calls are scary to the comfortable and inspiring to the hurting. Whichever group we are in, Mary's song reminds us: Jesus comes to *disrupt* our world. And in doing this, he saves us.

What prayers for justice do you pray? What pleas for justice are on others' hearts today?

During Advent, we long for peace on earth in the name of Jesus. But true peace, after all, entails true justice for all.

Prayer

Come, thou long-expected Jesus, born to set thy people free; / from our fears and sins release us; let us find our rest in thee. / Israel's strength and consolation, hope of all the earth thou art, / dear desire of ev'ry nation, joy of ev'ry longing heart. ("Come, thou long-expected Jesus," ELW 254)

December 15

Luke 1:54-56

"He has helped his servant Israel,
in remembrance of his mercy,
according to the promise he made to our ancestors,
to Abraham and to his descendants forever."
And Mary remained with [Elizabeth] about three months and
then returned to her home.

To ponder

O Lord, I have heard of your renown,
and I stand in awe, O Lord, of your work.
In our own time revive it; in our own time make it known;
in wrath may you remember mercy.—Habakkuk 3:2

God remembers you

Do you ever feel as if God has forgotten you? When things go wrong. When loved ones hurt you. When illness strikes. When you feel terribly lonely.

The people of Israel spent centuries feeling abandoned. Foreign nations conquered and ruled them. Their temple was ruined. And when a bid for independence succeeded, Rome conquered them shortly afterward. They could not help but ask: *God, have you completely forgotten us?*

Mary's song declares otherwise. In full view of age-old commitments, God has now come to Israel's aid, in remembrance and reenactment of mercy. To our ears, the words *help* and *remember* may not seem terribly impressive. But in scripture, when God remembers and helps people—like Noah, Rachel, Joseph, Hannah, Solomon, Hezekiah, and others—God steps in to redeem, to liberate, and to save.

Mary's child shows us that God does not forget God's people. More to the point, God will not forget about you. No matter how bleak your experience, God sees you, knows you, understands your hardships, and shows mercy.

You are not forgotten. You are not alone. God will not forsake you. The child Jesus stands as proof of that.

Prayer

Jesus, remember me when you come into your kingdom. Amen. (Luke 23:42)

December 16

Luke 1:57-58

Now the time came for Elizabeth to give birth, and she bore a son. Her neighbors and relatives heard that the Lord had shown his great mercy to her, and they rejoiced with her.

To ponder

Rejoice with those who rejoice, weep with those who weep.—Romans 12:15

Rejoicing in God's mercy

Luke promises to write an "orderly account" (1:3), but I want the messy, truer-to-our-complicated-lives account. Who was with Elizabeth when she gave birth to her long-awaited child? With her husband, Zechariah, rendered speechless, were there others who gently encouraged her to "push" and to "breathe"? Who ran from the room with the news of the baby's birth? How did the word spread? Was God's role in this miraculous birth obvious to all, or was there something in the witness that made it clear that this baby was an act of God's mercy?

During the long years of barrenness, did Elizabeth's neighbors and relatives weep with her? Did they pray with her and for her? Did they look for any reason—no matter how implausible—that would somehow reconcile their faith in God with this drawn-out tragedy? And were all those years of questioning, and perhaps even silent judgment, still in their minds when the good news of this baby's birth reached them?

Luke only tells us that Elizabeth's neighbors and relatives, hearing that the Lord had shown great mercy to her, rejoiced with her. And maybe that's enough. Whatever they had said *about* her, whatever they had tried to do *for* her . . . now they rejoiced *with* her.

Our lives can be so complicated. Our own insecurities can keep us from truly rejoicing when another experiences the gift of God's mercy. Today let's listen for good news in the lives of those around us and respond with wholehearted joy.

Prayer

God of great mercy, you invite us not only to weep with one another but to rejoice with one another. Open our ears to hear good news in the lives of others. Open our hearts to rejoice with our neighbors. Amen.

Luke 1:59-60, 63-64

On the eighth day they came to circumcise the child, and they were going to name him Zechariah after his father. But his mother said, "No; he is to be called John." . . . [Zechariah] asked for a writing tablet and wrote, "His name is John." And all of them were amazed. Immediately his mouth was opened and his tongue freed, and he began to speak, praising God.

To ponder

Let go of the narratives you've dragged around for years: you are not who you were as a child, or in year X, or on day Y—at least, not only. You do not have to fit yourself into those old, cramped stories. Be yourself here and now.—Maggie Smith, *Keep Moving*

Bold characters

Maybe Elizabeth always had it in her to say "no" when the time called for it. Or maybe she was newly empowered by the experience of God's mercy.

Maybe Zechariah always had it in him to stand up to the crowd. Or maybe he was transformed by the experience of being rendered speechless.

I don't imagine you're the same person you were as a child, or even the same person you were a year ago. God has been at work to empower and strengthen you, to shift your thinking, to give you courage. Maybe, like Elizabeth, now you can say "no" when necessary. Maybe, like Zechariah, now you can boldly proclaim God's praise.

God's intention was for this child, who would one day prepare the way for the coming Christ, to be named John. Could it be that God's dream was also for this baby's parents to revel in the new thing God was doing, not only through their newborn son, but through them?

What new thing is God doing in *you* this day?

Prayer

God who frees us for praise, inspire us to trade "old, cramped stories" for newly forming tales of your love shaping us. Made in your image, send us to be bold characters in your story of mercy for the world. Amen.

Luke 1:65-71

Fear came over all their neighbors, and all these things were talked about throughout the entire hill country of Judea. All who heard them pondered them and said, "What then will this child become?" ... Then his father Zechariah was filled with the Holy Spirit and spoke this prophecy:

"Blessed be the Lord God of Israel,
for he has looked favorably on his people and redeemed them.
He has raised up a mighty savior for us
in the house of his servant David,
as he spoke through the mouth of his holy prophets from of old,
that we would be saved from our enemies and from the hand of
all who hate us."

To ponder

Blessed be the One / who keeps on believing / in us / and blessed be the One / who goes on dreaming / in us / even when we forget.—Joyce Rupp, *Dear Heart, Come Home*

Blessed be God

The neighbors are talking: *What's happening? Who is this baby, born to Elizabeth and Zechariah? What will this child become?* Zechariah answers their questions. But first, he places his child in the context of a greater story. The answer to what this child will become begins with, and depends on, the God of Israel, the one who has already acted to save God's people.

Who John is to become, and who *we* are as God's people, begins with, and depends on, God. We're created, claimed, and called by the one whose purpose is to save the world, not to condemn it. We're held in the hands of the One who rescues us from hands that wish to harm us. We're held in the heart of the One who secures us from hearts that riddle us with hate.

Zechariah calls us to begin—again and again—by blessing this God. Praise God. Thank God. Recognize God at work in you and at work in the world. Bless the God who saves you daily, who believes in you without ceasing, who dreams in you even now.

Prayer

Blessed be you, O God, for looking on us with love. In these Advent days of expectation and yearning, help us to see anew the gift of your salvation. Amen.

December 19 / Advent 4

Luke 1:72-75

"Thus he has shown the mercy promised to our ancestors,
and has remembered his holy covenant,
the oath that he swore to our ancestor Abraham,
to grant us that we, being rescued from the hands of our enemies,
might serve him without fear, in holiness and righteousness
before him all our days."

To ponder

Those who can make us afraid have power over us. Those who make us live in a house of fear ultimately take our freedom away. . . . Wherever we live, the invitation of Christ beckons us to move out of the house of fear into the house of love: to leave our possessiveness for a place of freedom.—Henri J. M. Nouwen, *Turn My Mourning into Dancing*

Moving day

Zechariah's song goes on, shifting gracefully from the verse to the chorus, from the one to the many, from God to God's people, "that we, being rescued from the hands of our enemies, might serve [God] without fear."

What is the purpose of God saving us, redeeming us, remembering us? What happens when God keeps God's promise and rescues us, freeing us from all that threatens to demean and diminish us?

We serve God without fear. The end game is love of God and love of our neighbors. The point is a life of unrestrained service for the sake of the common good.

Are you living in a "house of fear" today? What's keeping you from doing what you know God has called you to do? What's boxing you in? What's stealing your courage? Today is moving day, beloved. God has made a way for you to move out of fear and into the freedom of wholehearted love. Thanks be to God!

Prayer

Thank you for bringing us to moving day, God. Help us to leave behind the fears that confine us to spaces too small for the abundance we know in you. Empower us to move with you into lives of boundless love. Amen.

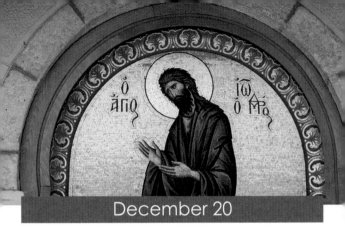

December 20

Luke 1:76-77

"And you, child, will be called the prophet of the Most High;
for you will go before the Lord to prepare his ways,
to give knowledge of salvation to his people
by the forgiveness of their sins."

To ponder

We are people who stand totally exposed before evil and death
and declare them powerless against love.—Rachel Held Evans,
Searching for Sunday

Job description

I recently had the great joy of baptizing a baby boy. Using the
words of the liturgy, I reminded the baby's parents of the respon-

sibilities they were taking on so that their child would learn to trust God, proclaim Christ through word and deed, care for others and the world God made, and work for justice and peace. At that moment, as if on cue, the baby yawned.

I wonder if baby John yawned too, when Zechariah shared John's particular tasks. Go before the Lord to prepare God's ways? Tell people about God's forgiveness and the gift of salvation? Can't you just imagine that newborn baby stretching his chubby arms to the heavens and opening his mouth in a wide yawn, as if to say, *Really? I'm tired just thinking about it!*

John's job description is overwhelming. *Our* job description is overwhelming! But we don't do the work alone. The God who calls us also equips us—freeing us, by way of forgiveness, to use the gifts we've been given.

John is to help God's people know that they're saved. But they won't know it if they're only called out for their bad behavior, or taken on a guilt trip. They'll know they're saved—they'll know they're loved—by the forgiveness of their sins.

This is how we proclaim Christ, how we care for the world, how we work for justice and peace—forgiven by God, we extend that same forgiveness to others. And together, forgiven and freed, our overwhelmed yawns turn to songs of joyful praise.

Prayer

Forgiving God, there are days when we feel stuck in judgment and resentment, frozen in shame and guilt. Thaw our hearts and minds with your abiding forgiveness. Amen.

December 21

Luke 1:78-79

"By the tender mercy of our God,
the dawn from on high will break upon us,
to give light to those who sit in darkness
and in the shadow of death,
to guide our feet into the way of peace."

To ponder

The good news of Christ crucified and risen had mighty power
in my life. It was the power of Christ to be present in any and
every situation, the power to bring life in the midst of death. This
gospel was everything to me, and I staked my life on it.—Renee
Splichal Larson, *A Witness*

The longest night

Zechariah saves the best for last. Those are the words I taped
to my office wall during a year when I was homesick not just for
home, but for the life I had known before the grief of my brother's
death. That is the promise to which I clung, the song I committed
to memory, the steady heartbeat of God that assured my weary
spirit that there was indeed a future with hope.

In the shadow of death the gospel we've known takes on new
urgency and renewed power. We need what we've trusted to be
true. We need to know there is light not only at the end of the
tunnel but in the very midst of this suffocating moment. We need
to know there is a way of peace already marked for us to travel.

This is a season of memory, when the losses through which
we've labored return at unexpected moments. With tender mercy
your God comes to you, dear one. You are not alone as you
grieve, as you weep, as you rage against the death that has tried to
destroy you. You are not alone as you pray, as you search, as you
struggle to believe.

The longest night will soon be over. The promised dawn will
rise. Your Savior is coming with healing in his wings.

Prayer

God of mercy, we need your tenderness to wipe away our tears.
Come to us now. Give us your light. Guide us to peace. Amen.

December 22

Luke 1:80

The child grew and became strong in spirit, and he was in the wilderness until the day he appeared publicly to Israel.

To ponder

Once upon a time, I thought a life of faith was a life of steady foundations and stable shores. Then I heard the unmistakable loon calling me out into the waters at night.—Sarah Bessey, *Miracles and Other Reasonable Things*

Wilderness child

The child is, of course, John. But it's curious that he's not named John here. He is simply "the child." It's as if Luke invites all of us, children of God, to grow and to become strong in the spirit, to spend time in the wilderness until we're ready for what comes next.

Luke tells us nothing of the child's growing years, of that wilderness time. Did the silence there help the child learn to listen for God's voice? Were the challenges there something akin to the struggles of God's people as they wandered in the wilderness after their time of slavery in Egypt? Did the child learn to look to God for manna? For water from the rock? Was this time in the wilderness something like Jesus' time there? Was it a time of temptation? A time of revealing? A time of formation? A time to be convicted of his purpose?

And what about you, child? Have you heard God calling you out into the waters at night? Have you spent time in the wilderness—far from the security of the familiar, the safety of the known? Have you met God there? Have you been fed by your Maker? Have you grown strong amid adversity, by experiencing God's powerful grasp on your life during the struggle? And now, child, what will *you* call out to a world in need? What good news will *you* proclaim?

Prayer

God of the wilderness, teach us to listen for you, to rely on you, to trust you above all else. Help us to grow and to become strong in spirit as we follow you into the unknown. Amen.

December 23

Luke 2:1-3

In those days a decree went out from Emperor Augustus that
all the world should be registered. This was the first registration
and was taken while Quirinius was governor of Syria. All went to
their own towns to be registered.

To ponder

God chose what is foolish in the world to shame the wise; God
chose what is weak in the world to shame the strong; God chose
what is low and despised in the world, things that are not, to
reduce to nothing things that are, so that no one might boast in
the presence of God.—1 Corinthians 1:27-29

Who really "counts"?

Luke's account of the birth of Jesus sets this holy event against a very human backdrop: the emperor taking stock of "all the world" under Roman rule. What are we to make of this?

The emperor's decree could explain why Mary and Joseph would chance a rigorous journey from Nazareth to Bethlehem so close to the birth of their child, traversing rocky hills and valleys in order to be counted. But that's not all. Luke's focus on the political events and people of "those days" also connects the birth of Jesus to human history, and to the human fixation on counting possessions, property, and people to determine who really "counts" in the scheme of things.

God enters the world as a newborn child: one of little account in terms of human power. In doing this, God takes the side of those who are discounted by human standards. In his birth, ministry, death, and resurrection, Jesus continually surprises and subverts human expectations, proclaiming God's reign as an uplifting of the lowly and a humbling of the powerful.

Where might we find God today in our midst, especially among those who are treated as though they do not count?

Prayer

God of the universe, your foolishness is wiser than our wisdom, and your weakness greater than our strength. Guide us to notice and care for those left out and unaccounted for, and remind us that we too are counted as precious in your sight. Amen.

Luke 2:4-5

Joseph also went from the town of Nazareth in Galilee to Judea, to the city of David called Bethlehem, because he was descended from the house and family of David. He went to be registered with Mary, to whom he was engaged and who was expecting a child.

To ponder

O little town of Bethlehem, how still we see thee lie! / Above thy deep and dreamless sleep the silent stars go by; / yet in thy dark streets shineth the everlasting light. / The hopes and fears of all the years are met in thee tonight.—"O little town of Bethlehem," ELW 279

Christmas present

For Joseph and Mary the road to Bethlehem was not only a journey of distance but also a journey of time. Joseph was returning to a place that was his ancestral homeland, but not his home. He was bringing the woman who would become—but was not yet—his wife. Into the birthplace of David, Israel's ancient king, Joseph and Mary carried a baby yet to be born, whose very existence would change the world forever.

As Joseph and Mary took each step toward Bethlehem, past and future collided in a moment we could call the *holy now*: a place of memory and of expectant hope. The "hopes and fears of all the years" met in the holy time between what once was and what would soon be.

When we retell the Christmas story each year, we tell it not as something that happened only "once upon a time" but as something that is *still happening* to us and to the world.

Like Joseph and Mary, we stand in the *holy now*, remembering God's promises of the past and hoping in God's promises for the future. In Joseph and Mary's journey, we find our own journey. Our hopes and fears are there too.

Prayer

God of our journeys, on this holy night you are again Immanuel, God with us. Rekindle our hope and faith in this *holy now*, that we may share the good news of your coming among us. Amen.

Luke 2:6-7

While they were there, the time came for her to deliver her child. And she gave birth to her firstborn son and wrapped him in bands of cloth, and laid him in a manger, because there was no place for them in the inn.

To ponder

Hark the glad sound! The Savior comes, the Savior promised long; / let ev'ry heart prepare a throne and ev'ry voice a song.— "Hark, the glad sound!," ELW 239

The glad sound

Our Christmas hymns often depict the birth of Jesus as quiet: a silent night, a still little town, and the world itself holding its breath to peer into the manger—where the "little Lord Jesus, no crying he makes."

In real life, childbirth is rarely silent. The work of bringing new life into the world is full of sounds: the groans of laboring, the encouraging murmurs of midwiving, the shuffles of feet and hands coming to bring aid. Today this might also include the beeps and clatters of a hospital delivery room; in Bethlehem on that long-ago night it perhaps included the snuffling and lowing of livestock. Then and now, amid it all, comes the piercing cry of an infant: the sound that means a new human being has drawn breath outside of the womb, has entered the world, has announced, "I am here!" The newborn baby's cry may be lusty or tentative, confused or demanding, but it is the very sound of life: a glad sound, indeed.

This Christmas may find us amid noise and bustle; or surrounded by quiet peace; or perhaps, sitting in the emptier silence of absence and loss. What is the glad sound in these times? How do we perceive it amid the world's many sounds and silences? How do we welcome the glad sound of the Savior's coming—and how do we answer?

Prayer

God of birth and beginnings, on Christmas Day came the glad sound of new life: Jesus, our Lord. Fill our hearts today with the joy of your presence, that our lives may become a song of your grace. Amen.

Luke 2:8-9

In that region there were shepherds living in the fields, keeping watch over their flock by night. Then an angel of the Lord stood before them, and the glory of the Lord shone around them, and they were terrified.

To ponder

The grace of God means something like . . . Here is the world. Beautiful and terrible things will happen. Don't be afraid. I am with you.—Frederick Buechner, *Beyond Words*

Fear and joy

Some fear is as far away from joy as it is possible to be: fear born of danger or of imagining the worst, fear stoked by listening to voices rooted in hatred rather than love, fear that makes us cling tightly to things we would be better off letting go. This fear is also known as terror.

Then there is the kind of fear that precedes great joy: fear that thrills us, from the tops of our heads to the tips of our toes; fear that makes our hearts beat faster in anticipation; fear that exhilarates us and makes us feel alive; fear that leaves our mouths slightly agape with wonder. This fear is also known as awe.

We do not know whether the sudden appearance of the angel of the Lord in the shepherds' fields inspired terror or awe—or perhaps a mixture of the two. We do know that, even in the shepherds' state of watchfulness, they were surprised and over-whelmed by the glory of the Lord shining in their midst. Who wouldn't be?

Perhaps this is a reminder that even when we are yearning for God to speak to us, it is not always comfortable or comforting when God actually shows up. And yet, we need not be afraid. God is with us; and where God is, even our terror can be trans-formed into joyful, jaw-dropping awe.

Prayer

God of glory, as your angel appeared to the shepherds, you still appear in our midst—and even when we are terrified, we are not alone. Turn all our fear to joy in your presence, that we may trust in you. Amen.

Luke 2:10-12

But the angel said to them, "Do not be afraid; for see—I am bringing you good news of great joy for all the people: to you is born this day in the city of David a Savior, who is the Messiah, the Lord. This will be a sign for you: you will find a child wrapped in bands of cloth and lying in a manger."

To ponder

I know of no God but this One in the manger.—Martin Luther, Christmas sermon, 1527

God in the manger

In the center of modern-day Bethlehem, the Church of the Nativity welcomes visitors from all over the world who bow their heads—in necessity as well as reverence—to enter the church through the "door of humility," a stone opening that stands only four feet high. It's a fitting entrance to a place that honors the God of the manger.

Martin Luther found great significance in the manger, and once likened the Bible itself to the manger: a work of human hands, made holy because Jesus Christ is found there. For Luther, it is not that God only exists in the manger, but that only the God of the manger can be the God of good news for all people: God for the poor and oppressed, not only for the privileged and powerful. The God of the manger, of course, is also the God of the cross, who defeats all the cosmic powers of sin and death through the humblest stuff of earth: straw and stone; water and bread; flesh and blood.

In the end, the manger reminds us that the gospel is not something we have to reach up to heaven to grasp. The gospel reaches down to us. It is already here, among us. This is good news of great joy indeed.

Prayer

God of the manger, you come to earth and fill it with your presence. Teach us to find you in the places of the manger and the cross, in our neighbors and our world, that we might receive and share your love and grace. Amen.

December 28

Luke 2:13-14

And suddenly there was with the angel a multitude of the heavenly host, praising God and saying, "Glory to God in the highest heaven, and on earth peace among those whom he favors!"

To ponder

Blessed is the season which engages the whole world in a conspiracy of love.—Hamilton Wright Mabie, *My Study Fire*

Breathing together

The word *conspiracy* contains the word *spirit*, which is the same word we use when we talk about breathing (for example, as in *respiration*). In scripture, God's spirit moves over the waters at creation and breathes life into all living things—including human beings. When we are inspired, it is as though God has breathed possibility and potential into us. When we aspire, we take in a deep breath, the better to propel us toward a goal—or to raise our voice in praise, proclamation, or peacemaking.

In a similar way, while we may think of conspiracy as an act of planning or plotting together, conspiracy could also mean something like *breathing together*. When I imagine heavenly multitudes praising God for the birth of Jesus, that's what I imagine: the angels and shepherds, rocks and grass, stars and dewdrops, filled with the breath of God and breathing together. I imagine all creation engaged in a conspiracy of life—and love.

When multitudes sing together, the melody is sustained even when a singer takes a breath. When multitudes conspire, the music carries us along even as we help to carry it. The heavenly host is a multitude. So is the communion of saints: the body of Christ, the church. Imagine the life of faith as community, as engaging in a conspiracy of love: breathing together a love strong enough to defeat fear and death, strong enough to reconcile all that is torn apart, strong enough to bring justice and peace to all the world. Imagine that each time we breathe, we breathe together with the God of the universe.

Prayer

God of inspiration, you are the breath of life, love, and hope for the world. Breathe into us, your people, that we may be filled with your Spirit and embody your love to all, in word and deed. Amen.

Luke 2:15-16

When the angels had left them and gone into heaven, the shepherds said to one another, "Let us go now to Bethlehem and see this thing that has taken place, which the Lord has made known to us." So they went with haste and found Mary and Joseph, and the child lying in the manger.

To ponder

Shepherds, why this jubilee? Why your joyous strains prolong? / What the gladsome tidings be which inspire your heavenly song? —"Angels we have heard on high," ELW 289

Jubilant shepherds

Staying with the sheep was the whole point. If the flocks didn't need watching, the shepherds could have slept in their own warm beds rather than keep awake in chilly fields. Yet in the afterglow of the angels, the shepherds wasted no time. They left their fields and hurried off to see for themselves the miraculous event that had taken place. Were the sheep left to graze alone? Or did the shepherds bring the whole baa-ing and bleating cacophony with them, awakening sleepy neighbors who asked: "Shepherds, why this jubilee?"

In the scriptures, "jubilee" is no ordinary celebration. It is "the year of the Lord's favor," an extraordinary time of freedom, homecoming, and forgiveness of debts. We can think of jubilee as a wonderful interruption of business as usual by something important enough to overtake everything else—like the end of a war. Or the birth of a child.

That Christmas night, the hymn imagines, jubilation came not only from the angels with their cascading glorias, but also from the shepherds themselves: singing joyous strains of heavenly song on the way to meet the child who would grow up to announce the year of the Lord's favor.

Prayer

God of jubilee, awaken us to your presence in the world, so that we might embrace your gospel with jubilation. Amen.

December 30

Luke 2:17-20

[The shepherds] made known what had been told them about this child; and all who heard it were amazed at what the shepherds told them. But Mary treasured all these words and pondered them in her heart. The shepherds returned, glorifying and praising God for all they had heard and seen.

To ponder

Do you see this grain of sand / Lying loosely in my hand? . . . / Can it be that God does care / For such atoms as we are? / Then outspake this grain of sand / "I was fashioned by [God's] hand / In the star lit realms of space / I was made to have a place." — Frances Ellen Watkins Harper, "A Grain of Sand"

Pondering, proclaiming, praising

The greatest and tiniest elements of the universe are equally miraculous: mountains and molecules, a far-off star or a grain of sand. Most of all, the newborn child who is also God incarnate—the creator of all, God-with-us.

How do we fit into this story of God's infinite and intimate love? Do we ponder like Mary, or proclaim like the shepherds? Should we pray inwardly, or praise outwardly? Stay at the manger, or go out into the world?

The manifold actions of the people around Jesus suggest that pondering, proclaiming, and praising are all important ways to respond to the good news. Perhaps this is a glimpse of another ordinary miracle, the community of faith—where pondering, proclamation, and praise are lifted up by a people diverse in gifts and callings, but one in Christ. Today I might need to ponder while you proclaim; tomorrow, I can praise as you ponder. When we join our faith together, like so many grains of sand or stars in the sky, we can be good news for a world in need of the reflection, reassurance, and renewal that the gospel brings.

Prayer

God of Mary and shepherds, sand and stars, you call us by name and invite us to ponder, proclaim, and praise your love. Draw us together in community and embolden us to be Christ's body in the world. Amen.

December 31

Luke 2:21

After eight days had passed, it was time to circumcise the child; and he was called Jesus, the name given by the angel before he was conceived in the womb.

To ponder

Make us die every day to sin so that we may rise to live with Christ forever.—Morning Prayer, *ELW*

Facing forward

We don't often think about the fact that Jesus was raised in the Jewish faith—that is, until we read a scripture passage like this one. Mary and Joseph brought their child to be circumcised, the practice that dates back in the Jewish faith to ancient times. They named their child Jesus, a name derived from a Hebrew word that means "God saves."

The Jewish practice of circumcision is a sign of God's promise to Abraham and his descendants. A circumcised child represents hope for the future—the future of the family, of the Jewish faith, and of God's continued blessings upon the world.

The early church came to the decision that circumcision would not be required of followers of Jesus, but individuals and sometimes entire households received the sacrament of baptism. This day, as we look ahead to a new year, is a good time to remember baptism. When we are baptized, we are named "children of God." We receive God's promises of forgiveness, new life, and the Holy Spirit. Through water and God's word, we die to sin and rise to new life in Christ. Baptism gives us a future filled with hope, God's unconditional love, and endless possibilities.

Prayer

God of our future, as our pasts have been reconciled into you, point our faces forward, in hope and expectation. Amen.

January 1

Luke 2:22-24

When the time came for their purification according to the law of Moses, they brought [Jesus] up to Jerusalem to present him to the Lord (as it is written in the law of the Lord, "Every firstborn male shall be designated as holy to the Lord"), and they offered a sacrifice according to what is stated in the law of the Lord, "a pair of turtledoves or two young pigeons."

To ponder

The horizon leans forward, offering you space to place new steps of change.—Maya Angelou, "On the Pulse of Morning"

An offering to God

As all Jewish parents did at that time, Mary and Joseph brought their firstborn son to the temple to be offered or dedicated to God. The wisdom of their faith taught them to honor God in everything they did. That faith included a provision for those who were poor to sacrifice doves, as Mary and Joseph did, instead of the customary lamb.

Today we move from one year into another, and social media will be fraught with messages like "So glad that year is over!" and "Can we just forget 2021 ever happened?" Meme after meme will be filled with these or similar sentiments, often speaking of time as if it's a person who's done us wrong. But if the pandemic and other events have taught us anything, it's that there are still reasons to be thankful, even during the most difficult times. So with some of the bright-eyed hopefulness of Mary and Joseph, let's begin this new year by giving thanks and offering God ourselves and all that we have—including the time that lies ahead of us. God has been with us in the past, and no matter what each day brings, God will be with us through it all.

Prayer

God of our past, present, and future, give us thankful hearts for your ongoing presence, hope for the promised future with you, and grace for the times when that is still too difficult for us. Amen.

Luke 2:25-26

Now there was a man in Jerusalem whose name was Simeon; this man was righteous and devout, looking forward to the consolation of Israel, and the Holy Spirit rested on him. It had been revealed to him by the Holy Spirit that he would not see death before he had seen the Lord's Messiah.

To ponder

The key to a good life is this: If you're not going to talk about something during the last hour of your life, then don't make it a top priority during your lifetime.—Richard Carlson, *Don't Sweat the Small Stuff*

Priorities

The older we get, the more our priorities change. No matter your age, I bet you have noticed that. In my twenties, I prioritized "stuff." By stuff I mean material things: electronics, car accessories, shoes—you know, stuff. By the time my thirties hit, I was more concerned with providing my kids with stuff than myself. And now in my mid-forties, I don't know what I want for Christmas anymore.

No one knows how old Simeon is in today's text, but it seems clear that he has lived long enough to make some big changes in his priorities. In fact, he has whittled those priorities down to one—just one. At this stage in his life he finds himself in the temple waiting to see the Messiah show up. There is a beautiful simplicity in that.

What if we made it a priority to see Jesus—in scripture, in prayer, in worship, in the sacraments—not only near the end of life but each day? And in doing that, wouldn't we want to help others to see Jesus too, by telling his story, loving and serving God and our neighbors, and working for justice and peace in the world? Maybe Simeon was onto something.

Prayer

God of our priorities, we want to see Jesus. Let others see him through us. Amen.

Luke 2:27-32

Guided by the Spirit, Simeon came into the temple. . . .
Simeon took [the child] in his arms and praised God, saying,
"Master, now you are dismissing your servant in peace,
according to your word; for my eyes have seen your salvation,
which you have prepared in the presence of all peoples,
a light for revelation to the Gentiles
and for glory to your people Israel."

To ponder

All of us go down to the dust, yet even at the grave we make our
song: Alleluia.—"All of us go down to the dust," ELW 223

In God's hands

"Now I've seen everything!" is a common refrain when we come across something quite extraordinary. We usually say it in jest, not intending for it to be taken literally. Simeon says something similar when he sees Jesus, but he means it! And now that he has seen the long-awaited Messiah, he can die in peace. The Savior has come, and his light shines not only for the people of Israel but for all the world.

As a pastor, I've had the privilege of walking life's final steps with many people. Some are clearly not ready. Others don't know what to think about the journey. Still others are afraid. Then there are people like Simeon, who are not only ready, but are content. This floors me every time I witness it.

Humans have a tendency to avoid talking about death, but as a pastor I often find myself nudging people to do just that. Not only is it healthy, but it also can make the present that much more meaningful. I like to think that because Simeon had thought about the end of his life, he was able to live each day to its fullest.

What do you want to witness or accomplish before your final days? Your life and death are in God's hands, dear reader. Make each day count.

Prayer

Gracious God, as we cling to the assurance that our end is in your hands, empower us to do your will today. Amen.

Luke 2:33-35

The child's father and mother were amazed at what was being said about him. Then Simeon blessed them and said to his mother Mary, "This child is destined for the falling and the rising of many in Israel, and to be a sign that will be opposed so that the inner thoughts of many will be revealed—and a sword will pierce your own soul too."

To ponder

Baby Jesus' mission seemed far away, / far from Bethlehem that day. / Baby breath gentle, warmed the room; / who knew that he would go from crib to cross so soon?—Rusty Edwards, "One Sacred Moment"

God so loved the world . . .

It must have been difficult at times for Mary and Joseph to keep their chins up. At every turn they seemed to encounter some kind of challenge, all because of the new addition to their family. They couldn't even have a simple ritual at the temple without some guy telling them how controversial their child would be, not to mention how painful things would be for them as parents.

How did Mary and Joseph react to this? Did they have second thoughts about raising this child? When you love someone—family member, friend, or stranger—you risk having your heart broken, because when they hurt, you hurt. When they break, you break. When they are persecuted, you are persecuted. So after presenting Jesus in the temple, Mary and Joseph returned to the town of Nazareth to raise their child.

God so loved the world that this holy child, God's only Son, was born in Bethlehem and laid in a manger. God's love for all people shined through Jesus' life and ministry. Then one day Jesus died on a cross and showed us God's love in a way no one ever had or ever will again.

Prayer

God of love, thank you for the incredible gift of your Son for the world. Amen.

Luke 2:36-38

There was also a prophet, Anna the daughter of Phanuel, of the tribe of Asher. She was of a great age. . . . She never left the temple but worshiped there with fasting and prayer night and day. At that moment she came and began to praise God and to speak about the child to all who were looking for the redemption of Jerusalem.

To ponder

Joy to the world, the Lord is come! Let earth receive her king; / let ev'ry heart prepare him room and heav'n and nature sing, / and heav'n and nature sing, and heav'n, and heav'n and nature sing.—"Joy to the world," ELW 267

Praise

When I was a child and something positive would happen, no matter how big or small, I remember my grandma saying, "Thank you, Jesus!" It wasn't a directive. She wasn't trying to convince anyone of anything. For her, it was just a fact, that whenever something positive happened, Jesus was worthy of praise and thanks. Period.

The prophet Anna hasn't gotten a lot of press over the last two thousand years. And that's too bad, because I think we all need an Anna in our lives. To be fair, the Simeons in our lives are helpful too. They are the ones who deliver the bad news along with the good. But then Anna comes along like a breath of fresh air, thanking and praising God and ready to celebrate with you.

Because of the Annas in my life, I have learned how to celebrate with people—especially those who are having a tough time finding something to celebrate. Who have been the Annas in your life? What kind of impact have they had on you? And how might you add more thanks and praise into your life and the lives of others?

Prayer

God of good news, give us hearts and hands that are always ready to praise you and celebrate your blessings. Amen.

January 6 / Epiphany of Our Lord

Luke 2:39-40

When they had finished everything required by the law of the Lord, they returned to Galilee, to their own town of Nazareth. The child grew and became strong, filled with wisdom; and the favor of God was upon him.

To ponder

Good Christian friends, rejoice with heart and soul and voice; / now ye need not fear the grave; Jesus Christ was born to save! / Calls you one and calls you all to gain the everlasting hall. / Christ was born to save! Christ was born to save!—"Good Christian friends, rejoice," ELW 288

Interconnectedness

On this day every year, members of our congregation travel to one another's homes to perform house blessings in remembrance of the magi's visit to little Jesus. This is one of our most intergenerational events of the year. It's an evening filled with smiles, laughter, singing, gift-giving, and prayer. Often a few tears are shed too. By the time we are done, we have seen firsthand just how interconnected we are within our faith community.

After all the events surrounding Jesus' birth, the new family was finally able to go home to live as normal a life as they could. We know little about these years in Nazareth, but Luke mentions that Jesus grew up and became strong and wise. (If this sounds somewhat familiar, look back at Luke 1:80.) Strength and wisdom are gifts received over time from a variety of sources. Jesus' strength and wisdom may have come from his parents, to be sure, but maybe also from his neighbors, relatives, teachers, or fellow carpenters.

An old adage says it takes a village to raise a child. Think back on your own upbringing. Who helped to raise you? Who told you about Jesus and nurtured your faith? And who have you helped to raise and to grow in faith?

Prayer

God who calls us, one and all, give us the strength and wisdom to see those around us as an interconnected web of life and love. Amen.

An evening service of light for Advent

This brief order may be used on any evening during the season of Advent. If the household has an Advent wreath (one candle for each of the four weeks of Advent), it may be lighted during this service. Alternatively, one simple candle (perhaps a votive candle) may be lighted instead.

Lighting the Advent wreath

May this candle/these candles be a sign of the coming light of Christ.

One or more candles may be lighted.

Week 1: Lighting the first candle

Blessed are you, God of Jacob, for you promise to transform weapons of war into implements of planting and harvest and to

teach us your way of peace; you promise that our night of sin is far gone and that your day of salvation is dawning.

As we light the first Advent candle, wake us from our sleep, wrap us in your light, empower us to live honorably, and guide us along your path of peace.

O house of Jacob, come,
let us walk in the light of the Lord. Amen.

Week 2: Lighting the first two candles
Blessed are you, God of hope, for you promise to bring forth a shoot from the stump of Jesse who will bring justice to the poor, who will deliver the needy and crush the oppressor, who will stand as a signal of hope for all people.

As we light these candles, turn our wills to bear the fruit of repentance, transform our hearts to live in justice and harmony with one another, and fix our eyes on the shoot from Jesse, Jesus Christ, the hope of all nations.

O people of hope, come,
let us rejoice in the faithfulness of the Lord. Amen.

Week 3: Lighting three candles
Blessed are you, God of might and majesty, for you promise to make the desert rejoice and blossom, to watch over the strangers, and to set the prisoners free.

As we light these candles, satisfy our hunger with your good gifts, open our eyes to the great things you have done for us, and fill us with patience until the coming of the Lord Jesus.

O ransomed people of the Lord, come,
let us travel on God's holy way
and enter into Zion with singing. Amen.

Week 4: Lighting all four candles
Blessed are you, God of hosts, for you promised to send a Son, Emmanuel, who brought your presence among us; and you promise through your Son Jesus to save us from our sin.

As we light these candles, turn again to us in mercy; strengthen our faith in the word spoken by your prophets; restore us and give us life that we may be saved.

O house of David, come,
let us rejoice, for the Son of God, Emmanuel,
comes to be with us. Amen.

Reading
Read the scripture passage printed in the devotion for the day.

Hymn
One of the following hymns may be sung. The hymn might be accompanied by small finger cymbals.

"Light one candle to watch for Messiah," ELW 240
"People, look east," ELW 248
"Savior of the nations, come," ELW 263

During the final seven days of the Advent season (beginning on December 17), the hymn "O come, O come, Emmanuel" (ELW 257) is particularly appropriate. The stanzas of that hymn are also referred to as the "O Antiphons." The first stanza of the hymn could be sung each day during the final days before Christmas in addition to the stanza that is specifically appointed for the day.

First stanza
O come, O come, Emmanuel,
and ransom captive Israel,
that mourns in lonely exile here
until the Son of God appear.
Refrain Rejoice! Rejoice! Emmanuel shall come to you, O Israel.

December 17
O come, O Wisdom from on high,
embracing all things far and nigh:
in strength and beauty come and stay;
teach us your will and guide our way. *Refrain*

December 18
O come, O come, O Lord of might,
as to your tribes on Sinai's height
in ancient times you gave the law
in cloud, and majesty, and awe. *Refrain*

December 19

O come, O Branch of Jesse, free
your own from Satan's tyranny;
from depths of hell your people save,
and give them vict'ry o'er the grave. *Refrain*

December 20

O come, O Key of David, come,
and open wide our heav'nly home;
make safe the way that leads on high,
and close the path to misery. *Refrain*

December 21

O come, O Dayspring, come and cheer;
O Sun of justice, now draw near.
Disperse the gloomy clouds of night,
and death's dark shadow put to flight. *Refrain*

December 22

O come, O King of nations, come,
O Cornerstone that binds in one:
refresh the hearts that long for you;
restore the broken, make us new. *Refrain*

December 23

O come, O come, Emmanuel,
and ransom captive Israel,
that mourns in lonely exile here
until the Son of God appear. *Refrain*

Text: *Psalteriolum Cantionum Catholicarum*, Köln, 1710; tr. composite
Text sts. 2, 6, 7 © 1997 Augsburg Fortress

Table prayer for Advent

Blessed are you, O Lord our God,
the one who is, who was, and who is to come.
At this table you fill us with good things.
May these gifts strengthen us
to share with the hungry and all those in need,
as we wait and watch for your coming among us
in Jesus Christ our Lord. Amen.

Lighting the Christmas tree

Use this prayer when you first illumine the tree or when you gather at the tree.

Holy God,
we praise you as we light this tree.
It gives light to this place
as you shine light into darkness through Jesus,
the light of the world.

God of all,
we thank you for your love,
the love that has come to us in Jesus.
Be with us now as we remember that gift of love,
and help us to share that love with a yearning world.

Creator God,
you made the stars in the heavens.
Thank you for the light that shines on us in Jesus,
the bright morning star.
Amen.

Blessing of the nativity scene

This blessing may be used when figures are added to the nativity scene and throughout the days of Christmas.

Bless us, O God, as we remember a humble birth. With each angel and shepherd we place here before you, show us the wonder found in a stable. In song and prayer, silence and awe, we adore your gift of love, Christ Jesus our Savior. Amen.

Table prayer for the twelve days of Christmas (December 25–January 5)

With joy and gladness we feast upon your love, O God.
You have come among us in Jesus, your Son,
and your presence now graces this table.
May Christ dwell in us
that we might bear his love to all the world,
for he is Lord forever and ever. Amen.

Blessing for a home at Epiphany

Matthew writes that when the magi saw the shining star stop overhead, they were filled with joy. "On entering the house, they saw the child with Mary his mother" (Matthew 2:11). In the home, Christ is met in family and friends, in visitors and strangers. In the home, faith is shared, nurtured, and put into action. In the home, Christ is welcome.

Twelfth Night (January 5), Epiphany of Our Lord (January 6), or another day during the time after Epiphany offers an occasion for gathering with friends and family members for a blessing of the home. Someone may lead the greeting and blessing, while another person may read the scripture passage. Following an Eastern European tradition, a visual blessing may be inscribed with white chalk above the main door; for example, 20 + CMB + 22. The numbers change with each new year. The three letters stand for either the ancient Latin blessing Christe mansionem benedicat, *which means "Christ, bless this house," or the legendary names of the magi (Caspar, Melchior, and Balthasar).*

Greeting

Peace to this house and to all who enter here.
By wisdom a house is built,
and through understanding it is established;
through knowledge its rooms are filled
with rare and beautiful treasures. (Prov. 24:3-4)

Reading

As we prepare to ask God's blessing on this household,
let us listen to the words of scripture.

In the beginning was the Word,
and the Word was with God, and the Word was God.
He was in the beginning with God.
All things came into being through him,
and without him not one thing came into being.
What has come into being in him was life,
and the life was the light of all people.
The Word became flesh and lived among us, and we have seen
   his glory,
the glory as of a father's only son, full of grace and truth.
From his fullness we have all received, grace upon grace.
(*John 1:1-4, 14, 16*)

Inscription

This inscription may be made with chalk above the entrance:
20 + C M B + 22

Write the appropriate character (left) while speaking the text (right).
The magi of old, known as

C	Caspar,
M	Melchior, and
B	Balthasar,

followed the star of God's Son who came to dwell among us

20	two thousand
22	and twenty-two years ago.
+	Christ, bless this house,
+	and remain with us throughout the new year.

Prayer of Blessing

O God,

you revealed your Son to all people by the shining light of a star.
We pray that you bless this home and all who live here
with your gracious presence.
May your love be our inspiration, your wisdom our guide,
your truth our light, and your peace our benediction;
through Christ our Lord. Amen.

*Then everyone may walk from room to room, blessing the house with
incense or by sprinkling with water, perhaps using a branch from the
Christmas tree.*

Table prayer for Epiphany

Generous God,

you have made yourself known in Jesus, the light of the world.
As this food and drink give us refreshment,
so strengthen us by your spirit,
that as your baptized sons and daughters
we may share your light with all the world.
Grant this through Christ our Lord.
Amen.

Notes

November 28: Richard Rohr, "Truth Is One," Center for Action and Contemplation, November 22, 2016, https://cac.org/truth-is-one-2016-11-22/. **November 29:** Rachel Held Evans, *A Year of Biblical Womanhood* (Nashville: Nelson, 2012). **November 30:** Charlotte Clemensen Taylor, "Former Chaplain Working to Found First New Order of Monks in 700 Years," *The Salina Journal*, January 10, 1986. **December 1:** Malcolm Guite, "As If," *Parable and Paradox* (London: Canterbury, 2016). **December 2:** Barbara Brown Taylor, *An Altar in the World* (New York: HarperCollins, 2010). **December 3:** Anne Lamott, *Traveling Mercies* (New York: Pantheon, 2000). **December 4:** Joseph Campbell, Bill Moyers, *The Power of Myth* (New York: Anchor, 1991). **December 5:** Martin Luther, letter no. 1610 to Justus Jonas the Elder, June 29, 1530, *WA Briefe* V, 409. **December 6:** Mary Oliver, "The World I Live In," *Devotions* (New York: Penguin, 2020), 5. **December 7:** Henri J. M. Nouwen, *Life of the Beloved* (New York: Crossroad, 2002), 31, 33. **December 8:** Martin Luther King Jr., "Speech at Bishop Charles Mason Temple," April 3, 1968, Memphis, TN. *Psalteriolum Cantionum Catholicarum*, Köln, 1710; tr. composite, "O come, O come, Emmanuel," ELW 257, st. 7 and refrain, text © 1997 Augsburg Fortress. **December 9:** Mary Oliver, "Evidence (1)," *Evidence* (Boston: Beacon, 2009), 43–46. **December 10:** Henri J. M. Nouwen, *In the Name of Jesus* (New York: Crossroad, 1989), 81. Thomas Merton, *Thoughts in Solitude* (New York: Abbey of Our Lady of Gethsemani, 1958). **December 11:** C. S. Lewis, *Letters to Malcolm* (San Diego: Harvest, 1964), 93. **December 12:** St. Augustine of Hippo, *Sermons* 4.1.1. **December 13:** St. Augustine, "Exposition of the Psalms" 72:1 (writer's translation), paragraph 1156, *Catechism of the Catholic Church* (Vatican Library, 1993), accessible at www.vatican.va/archive/ccc/index.htm. *With One Voice*, 1995, based on the Magnificat, "My soul proclaims your greatness," ELW 251, st. 1, text © 1995 Augsburg Fortress. **December 14:** Martin Luther King Jr., "When Peace Becomes Obnoxious" (sermon), March 18, 1956, Montgomery, AL, https://kinginstitute.stanford.edu/king-papers/documents/when-peace

-becomes-obnoxious. Charles Wesley, 1707–1788, "Come, thou long-expected Jesus," ELW 254, st. 1. **December 17:** Maggie Smith, *Keep Moving* (New York: One Signal Publishers/Atria, 2020), 148. **December 18:** Joyce Rupp, *Dear Heart, Come Home* (New York: Crossroad, 1996), 139–140. **December 19:** Henri J. M. Nouwen, *Turn My Mourning into Dancing* (Nashville: Word, 2001), 32–33. **December 20:** Rachel Held Evans, *Searching for Sunday* (Nashville: Nelson, 2015), 22. **December 21:** Renee Splichal Larson, *A Witness* (Eugene: Wipf & Stock, 2016), 119. **December 22:** Sarah Bessey, *Miracles and Other Reasonable Things* (New York: Howard/Atria, 2019), 206. **December 24:** Phillips Brooks, 1835–1893, "O little town of Bethlehem," ELW 279, st. 1. **December 25:** Philip Doddridge, 1702–1751, "Hark, the glad sound!," ELW 239, st. 1. **December 26:** Frederick Buechner, *Beyond Words* (New York: HarperOne, 2004), 139. **December 27:** Martin Luther, Christmas sermon, 1527, *WA*, 23:731. **December 28:** Hamilton Wright Mabie, *My Study Fire*, reprint ed. (Norderstedt, Schleswig-Holstein, Germany: Hansebooks, 2017). **December 29:** French carol; tr. H. F. Hemy, The Crown of Jesus Music, 1864, "Angels we have heard on high," ELW 289, st. 2. **December 30:** Frances Ellen Watkins Harper (1825–1911), "A Grain of Sand," https://poets.org/poem/grain-sand. **December 31:** Morning Prayer, *ELW*, p. 308. **January 1:** Maya Angelou, "On the Pulse of Morning," *New York Times*, January 21, 1993. **January 2:** Richard Carlson, *Don't Sweat the Small Stuff . . . and It's All Small Stuff* (New York: Hyperion, 1997). **January 3:** "All of us go down to the dust," ELW 223. **January 4:** Rusty Edwards, "One Sacred Moment," *As Sunshine to a Garden*, refrain. © 1999 Augsburg Fortress. **January 5:** Isaac Watts, 1674–1748, "Joy to the world," ELW 267, st. 1. **January 6:** Medieval Latin carol; tr. John Mason Neale, 1818–1866, "Good Christian friends, rejoice," ELW 288, st. 3.